Cocktail

COCK and MORE!

Everything you need to know about Cocktail mixes

By:

Les Ilagan

No part of this book may be reproduced, scanned, or distributed in any printed or electronic form without permission. Please do not participate or encourage piracy of copyrighted materials in violation of the author's rights. Purchase only authorized editions.

Copyright © by Les Ilagan

All Rights Reserved

Les Ilagan

Copyright © CONTENT ARCADE PUBLISHING. All rights reserved.

This cookbook is copyright protected and meant for personal use only.

No part of this cookbook may be used, paraphrased, reproduced, scanned, distributed or sold in any printed or electronic form without permission of the author and the publishing company. Copying pages or any part of this book for any purpose other than own personal use is prohibited and would also mean violation of copyright law

DISCLAIMER

Content Arcade Publishing and its authors are joined together in their efforts in creating these pages and their publications. Content Arcade Publishing and its authors make no assurance of any kind, stated or implied, with respect to the information provided.

LIMITS OF LIABILITY

Content Arcade Publishing and its authors shall not be held legally responsible in the event of incidental or consequential damages in line with, or arising out of, the supplying of the information presented here.

Les Ilagan

Table of Contents

DISCLAIMER 3

Introduction 5

Margarita Recipes 11

Frozen Strawberry Margarita Recipe................11

Fresh Pineapple and Lime Margarita Recipe 15

Cranberry Lime Margarita Recipe......................17

Coconut Lime MargaritaRecipe 19

Frozen Kiwi and Lime MargaritaRecipe............21

Luscious Mango MargaritaRecipe 25

Frozen Raspberry and Lime Margarita Recipe .27

Extremely Delicious MargaritaRecipe 31

Easy Cranberry Martini Recipe 36

Fruity MartiniRecipe 43

Honey Lemon MartiniRecipe.............................47

The Original Long Island Iced TeaRecipe 63

The Best Manhattan CocktailRecipe..................65

Easy Scotch Manhattan CocktailRecipe.............67

INTRODUCTION

This book gives you a collection of fantastic cocktail recipes, both alcoholic and non-alcoholic mixes.

Cocktails are normally served during parties and special occasions. It can either give you a refreshing feeling or warm you up as the day or night goes by. Surely, these special drinks will bring life to any party!

This recipe book include few basic bartending tips and a wide selection of great tasting and wonderful cocktail mixes that you can choose from. They are very easy to follow that even beginners can do it themselves, provided that you have the right ingredients and equipment needed.

Now, you don't have to go to a bar and celebrate! You can bring the bar to your home by following the cocktail recipes in this book. Your friends will surely be amazed with your new learned skill and enjoy every sip of their cocktail mixes!

Do's and Don'ts of Making Fantastic Cocktails

Cocktails are a great treat especially at parties or whenever you are entertaining guests. Summer is also the perfect time to make some refreshing drinks. But sometimes we find it difficult to get the desired results. Creating your own perfect cocktails would take a bit of practice and some bartending skills that can easily be learned. Here are some tips to guide you when doing cocktail mixes:

1. Small is Better.
When buying bottled sodas, choose the smallest bottles available unless you are using them in one occasion, say you have a party. Soda is a carbonated beverage and the most of the carbonation is lost when the seal is opened which might give your cocktail mixture a flat and

undesirable taste when you use a day old soda.

2. Shaking vs. Stirring.
Shaking is done when adding thick liquids like fruit juices, dairy, cream liqueur, and syrup. While stirring is for drinks that makes use of very light liquids or mixer like distilled spirits – gin and whiskey.

3. Ice should come First.
When shaking, put the ice first halfway onto a cocktail shaker, this will help chill the shaker and cool the mixers as you add them.

4. Just Enough!
Do not over fill your shaker. Doing so, will cause the mixture to spill and the mixers will have not much room to move around and mix properly.

5. Shake it Baby!
When the recipe calls for a cocktail shaker. This would also mean that you have to shake it hard and long. Because

some ingredients are thicker than others that will require longer time and also it will create better texture - "frosty".

6. Blend It!
When using a blender it is best to process first the fruits, juices and other mixers or liquids. This will ensure that the mixture is smooth before you add the ice and blend further.

7. When to Skip Sodas?
If using the blender, better skip the soda or any other carbonated beverage. Doing so, will create a big mess on your bar table for sure.

8. When do we Strain?
Straining is done when you want a clear cocktail or free from any sediments like torn mint, fruit pulp, and the like.

9. Always go for Quality.
When buying your ingredients, always choose fresh and those that have high

quality. This will make a great impact on the taste of your cocktails.

10. Hot and Cold

Use chilled glasses for cold drinks and warm glass for hot drinks. It will hold the desired temperature of the drink for longer period.

11. Garnishes have some use too.

The garnishes like lime or lemon in *Gin and Tonic* give its signature citrus flavor. While, the olives in *Martini* gives that briny flavor.

12. Measure Up!

Measuring your cocktail ingredients is essential to give you your desired taste because it balances the flavor of your mixers. If you don't measure, you will most likely not get the same results on your next batches.

Margarita Recipes

Frozen Strawberry Margarita Recipe

This seems to be the most loved flavored margarita of all time!

Preparation Time: 5minutes
Total Time: 5 minutes
Yield: 2 servings

Ingredients
1 ½ cup fresh or frozen strawberries
1 cup crushed ice
¼ cup tequila
¼ cup lime juice
2 Tbsp. orange-flavored liqueur

Method
1. Combine the strawberries, crushed ice, tequila, lime juice, and liqueur in a blender. Process until smooth.
2. Pour in margarita glasses. Garnish with strawberry or a slice of lime, if desired.
3. Serve and enjoy.

Frozen Pine Orange Margarita Recipe

This frozen margarita has a nice tropical flavor from the pineapple and orange.

Preparation Time: 5 minutes
Total Time: 5 minutes
Yield: 2 servings

Ingredients

1 cup crushed ice
1/2 cup pineapple juice
1/4 cup tequila
1/3 cup orange juice
2 Tbsp. orange liqueur
2 Tbsp. simple syrup

Method

1. Combine the crushed ice, pineapple juice, tequila, orange juice, liqueur, and syrup in a blender. Process until smooth.
2. Pour in margarita glasses. Garnish with small slice of pineapple, if desired.
3. Serve and enjoy.

Fresh Pineapple and Lime Margarita Recipe

This is a great margarita recipe, perfect treat when the weather gets hot!

Preparation Time: 5 minutes
Total Time: 5 minutes
Yield: 2 servings

Ingredients
1 ½ cups fresh pineapple chunks
¼ cup tequila
¼ cup lime juice
2 Tbsp. orange liqueur
2 Tbsp. simple syrup
¾ cup crushed ice

Method
1. Combine the pineapple chunks, tequila, lime juice, liqueur, and syrup in a blender. Process until smooth. Add the ice and blend further for another 20-30 seconds.
2. Pour in margarita glasses. Garnish with slice of lime or pineapple, if desired.
3. Serve and enjoy.

Cranberry Lime Margarita Recipe

This margarita recipe with cranberry and lime is very tasty!

Preparation Time: 5 minutes
Total Time: 5 minutes
Yield: 2 servings

Ingredients
1 cup crushed ice
2/3 cup cranberry juice
1/4 cup fresh lime juice
1/4 cup tequila
2 Tbsp. orange liqueur (Cointreau)
2 Tbsp. grenadine

Method
1. Combine the crushed ice, cranberry juice, lime juice, tequila, liqueur, and grenadine in a blender. Process until smooth.
2. Pour in margarita glasses. Garnish with mint sprig.
3. Serve and enjoy.

Coconut Lime Margarita Recipe

This margarita recipe with coconut milk is simply irresistible!

Preparation Time: 5 minutes
Total Time:5 minutes
Yield:2 servings

Ingredients
¼ cup sweet and sour mix
¼ cup tequila
½ cup coconut milk
¼ cup lime juice
2 Tbsp. triple sec
1 cup crushed ice
green-colored sugar, to rim the glass (optional)

Method
1. Combine the sweet and sour mix, tequila, coconut milk, lime juice, triple sec, and crushed ice in a blender. Process until smooth.
2. Pour in margarita glasses. Garnish with a slice of lime.
3. Serve and enjoy.

Frozen Kiwi and Lime Margarita Recipe

This is a very delicious cocktail made of fresh kiwi and lime.

Preparation Time: 5 minutes
Total Time: 5 minutes
Yield: 2 servings

Ingredients

2 medium kiwi fruit, sliced
¼ cup fresh lime juice
¼ cup tequila
¼ cup triple sec
2 Tbsp. simple syrup
1 cup crushed ice
sugar granules, to rim the glasses

Method

1. Rim the chilled margarita glasses by dipping in lime juice then sugar.
2. Combine the kiwi, lime juice, tequila, triple sec, and syrup in a blender. Process until smooth. Add the crush ice and blend further 20-30 seconds.
3. Pour in margarita glasses. Garnish with a slice of lime.
4. Serve and enjoy.

Frozen Citrus Margarita Recipe

This is a very simple drink to make, yet taste really great.

Preparation Time: 5 minutes
Total Time: 5 minutes
Yield: 2 servings

Ingredients
1 oz. lemonade concentrate
1 oz. limeade concentrate
½ cup chilled club soda
¼ cup tequila
¼ cup triple sec
1 Tbsp. simple syrup
1 cup crushed ice
salt or sugar, to rim the glasses

Method
1. Rim the chilled glasses by dipping in lime juice then salt or sugar.
2. Combine the lemonade concentrate, limeade concentrate, club soda, tequila, triple sec, and syrup in a mixing glass. Stir well.
3. Pour in glasses with crushed ice.
4. Serve and enjoy.

Luscious Mango Margarita Recipe

This margarita with mango is the perfect drink for shower parties!

Preparation Time: 5 minutes
Total Time: 5 minutes
Yield: 1 serving

Ingredients

½ cup mango nectar or mango puree
1 oz. tequila
1 oz. lime juice
2 Tbsp. triple sec
1 Tbsp. simple syrup
¾ cup ice cubes
salt or sugar, to rim the glasses

Method

1. Rim the chilled glasses by dipping in lime juice then salt or sugar.
2. Place mango nectar, tequila, lime juice, triple sec, and syrup in a cocktail shaker. Shake for 10-15 seconds.
3. Pour in chilled glasses with ice cubes. Garnish with a slice of mango or lime, if desired.
4. Serve and enjoy.

Frozen Raspberry and Lime Margarita Recipe

This is an amazing cocktail recipe. You can serve this during special occasions and your friends will surely love it.

Preparation Time: 5 minutes
Total Time: 5 minutes
Yield: 2 servings

Ingredients

1 ½ cup fresh or frozen raspberries
1 cup crushed ice
¼ cup tequila
¼ cup fresh lime juice
2 Tbsp. orange liqueur
2 Tbsp. simple syrup

Method

1. Combine raspberries, crushed ice, tequila, liqueur, and syrup in a blender. Process until smooth.
2. Pour in chilled glasses. Garnish with a slice of lime, if desired.
3. Serve and enjoy.

Classic Margarita on the Rocks Recipe

This classic margarita recipe is simple yet so delicious.

Preparation Time: 5 minutes
Total Time: 5 minutes
Yield: 2 servings

Ingredients

¼ cup sweet and sour mix
1 ½ jigger tequila
1 ½ jigger lime juice
2 Tbsp. triple sec
1 Tbsp. simple syrup
1 cup ice cubes
salt or sugar, to rim the glasses

Method

1. Rim the chilled glasses by dipping in lime juice then salt or sugar.
2. Place sweet and sour mix, tequila, lime juice, triple sec, and syrup in a cocktail shaker. Shake for 10-15 seconds.
3. Pour in chilled glasses with ice cubes. Garnish with a slice of lime, if desired.
4. Serve and enjoy.

Extremely Delicious Margarita Recipe

This awesome margarita is a sure hit at parties!

Preparation Time: 5 minutes
Total Time: 5 minutes
Yield: 2 servings

Ingredients
¾ cup ice cubes
¼ cup gold tequila
¼ cup good quality lager-style beer
¼ cup freshly squeezed lime juice
2Tbsp. orange-flavored liqueur
2 Tbsp. triple sec
1 tsp. simple syrup
coarse salt, to rim the glasses

Method
1. Rim the chilled glasses by dipping in lime juice then salt.
2. Place ice cubes, tequila, beer, lime juice, liqueur, triple sec, and syrup in a cocktail shaker. Shake for 10-15 seconds.
3. Strain and pour in chilled glasses. Garnish with a slice of lime, if desired.
4. Serve and enjoy.

Citrus Moonshine Margarita Recipe

This margarita recipe tastes great and it only takes a few minutes to prepare.

Preparation Time: 5 minutes
Total Time: 5 minutes
Yield: 2 servings

Ingredients
¾ cup ice cubes
¼ cup tequila
¼ cup moonshine
¼ cup fresh lemon juice
2 Tbsp. orange-flavored liqueur
1 Tbsp. simple syrup
sugar, to rim the glasses

Method
1. Rim the chilled glasses by dipping in lemon juice then sugar.
2. Place ice cubes, tequila, moonshine, lemon juice, liqueur, and syrup in a cocktail shaker. Shake for 10-15 seconds.
3. Strain and pour in chilled glasses. Garnish with a slice of lemon, if desired.
4. Serve and enjoy.

Easy Orange Margarita Recipe

Try this orange margarita recipe on your next gathering, so yummy and refreshing!

Preparation Time: 5 minutes
Total Time: 5 minutes
Yield: 2 servings

Ingredients

¾ cup ice cubes
¼ cup gold tequila
¼ cup fresh orange juice
2 Tbsp. lemon juice
2 Tbsp. orange-flavored liqueur
1 Tbsp. simple syrup
salt, to rim the glasses

Method

1. Rim the chilled glasses by dipping in lemon juice then salt.
2. Place ice cubes, tequila, orange juice, lemon juice, liqueur, and syrup in a cocktail shaker. Shake for 10-15 seconds.
3. Strain and pour in chilled glasses. Garnish with a slice of orange or lemon, if desired.
4. Serve and enjoy.

<u>Martini Recipes</u>

Easy Cranberry Martini Recipe

The cranberry juice adds a nice twist to the classic martini recipe.

Preparation Time: 5 minutes
Total Time: 5 minutes
Yield: 2 servings

Ingredients
2 jiggers cranberry juice
1 jigger vodka
½ jigger dry vermouth
½ jigger orange liqueur
1 cup ice cubes

Method
1. Place the ice cubes, cranberry juice, vodka, vermouth, and liqueur in a cocktail shaker. Shake for 10-15 seconds.
2. Strain and pour in chilled glasses. Garnish with a slice of lime, if desired.
3. Serve and enjoy.

◆◆◆◆◆◆◆◆

Apple Lime Martini Recipe

This cocktail recipe is perfect for all martini lovers!

Preparation Time: 5 minutes
Total Time: 5 minutes
Yield: 2 servings

Ingredients
1 cup ice cubes
1 jigger apple schnapps
1 jigger vodka
1 jigger lime soda
½ jigger dry vermouth

Method

1. Combine the ice cubes, apple schnapps, vodka, and lime soda, and vermouth in a cocktail shaker. Shake vigorously for 10-15 seconds.
2. Strain and pour in chilled glasses. Garnish with a slice of apple, if desired.
3. Serve and enjoy.

◆◆◆◆◆◆◆◆◆

Pineapple Lemon Martini Recipe

Treat yourself with this delightful cocktail with pineapple and lemon.

Preparation Time: 5 minutes
Total Time: 5 minutes
Yield: 2 servings

Ingredients
1 cup ice cubes
2 jigger pineapple juice
1 jigger vodka
1 jigger frozen lemonade
½ jigger orange liqueur

Method
1. Combine the ice cubes, pineapple juice, vodka, lemonade, and liqueur in a cocktail shaker. Shake vigorously for 10-15 seconds.
2. Strain and pour in chilled glasses. Garnish with mint sprig, if desired.
3. Serve and enjoy.

♦♦♦♦♦♦♦♦

Fruity Martini Recipe

This martini recipe with grapefruit juice and apple juice is so delicious and refreshing.

Preparation Time: 5 minutes
Total Time: 5 minutes
Yield: 2 servings

Ingredients
1 cup ice cubes
2 jigger pink grapefruit juice
1 jigger apple juice
1 jigger vodka
½ jigger orange liqueur

Method
1. Combine the ice cubes, grapefruit juice, apple juice, vodka, and liqueur in a cocktail shaker. Shake vigorously for 10-15 seconds.
2. Strain and pour in chilled glasses. Garnish with a slice of apple or grapefruit, if desired.
3. Serve and enjoy.

◆◆◆◆◆◆◆◆

Frozen Raspberry and Orange Martini Recipe

If you are looking for a great tasting drink to serve your guests, this is the recipe for you!

Preparation Time: 5 minutes
Total Time: 5 minutes
Yield: 2 servings

Ingredients
1 cup fresh raspberries
2 jigger vodka
1 jigger orange juice
½ jigger dry vermouth
¾ cup crushed ice

Method
1. Combine the raspberries, vodka, orange juice, vermouth, and crushed ice in a blender. Process until smooth.
2. Pour in chilled glasses. Garnish with raspberry or orange rind, if desired.
3. Serve and enjoy.

◆◆◆◆◆◆◆◆

Honey Lemon Martini Recipe

This refreshing lemon martini recipe is perfect on any occasion.

Preparation Time: 5 minutes
Total Time: 5 minutes
Yield: 2 servings

Ingredients
1 cup ice cubes
2 jigger vodka
1 jigger lemon juice
½ jigger orange liqueur
1 Tbsp. honey

Method
1. Combine the ice cubes, vodka, lemon juice, and liqueur in a cocktail shaker. Shake vigorously for 10-15 seconds.
2. Strain and pour in chilled glasses. Garnish with a slice of lemon, if desired.
3. Serve and enjoy.

◆◆◆◆◆◆◆◆◆

Pink Blush Martini Recipe

This martini recipe is so yummy, it makes a great refreshment when the weather is hot.

Preparation Time: 5 minutes
Total Time: 5 minutes
Yield: 2 servings

Ingredients
1 cup ice cubes
2 jigger cranberry juice
1 jigger peach schnapps
1 jigger vodka
½ jigger lime juice
½ jigger triple sec

Method
1. Place the ice cubes, cranberry juice, peach schnapps, vodka, lime juice, and triple sec in a cocktail shaker. Shake vigorously for 10-15 seconds.
2. Strain and pour in chilled glasses. Garnish with a slice of lime, if desired.
3. Serve and enjoy.

♦♦♦♦♦♦♦♦

Frozen Watermelon Martini Recipe

This wonderful martini recipe with watermelon is the best summer drink ever!

Preparation Time: 5 minutes
Total Time: 5 minutes
Yield: 2 servings

Ingredients
1 cup watermelon
2 jigger vodka
1 jigger lime juice
½ jigger dry vermouth
¾ cup crushed ice

Method
1. Combine the watermelon, vodka, lime juice, vermouth, and crushed ice in a blender. Process until smooth.
2. Pour in chilled glasses. Garnish with a small slice of watermelon, if desired.
3. Serve and enjoy.

♦♦♦♦♦♦♦♦♦

All-Time Favorite Cocktail Recipes

Lovely Tequila Sunrise Recipe

This fantastic tequila cocktail recipe is surely everybody's favorite!

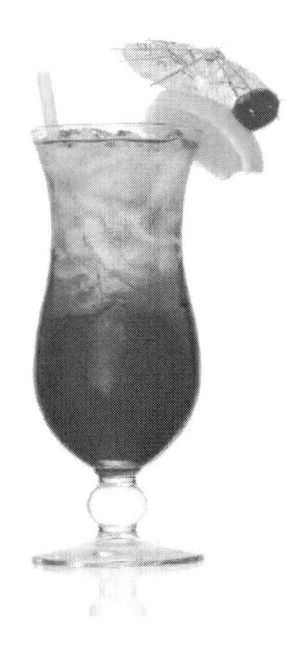

Preparation Time: 5 minutes
Total Time: 5 minutes
Yield: 1 serving

Ingredients
2 jiggers fresh orange juice, chilled
1 jigger gold tequila
1 ½ Tbsp. grenadine syrup
2/3 cup ice cubes

Method
1. Mix together orange juice and tequila in a chilled glass. Add grenadine syrup, let it settle at the bottom, then add the ice cubes.
2. Garnish with a slice of orange and cherry, if desired. Serve without stirring.
3. Enjoy.

♦♦♦♦♦♦♦♦♦

Frozen Pina Colada Recipe

This cocktail recipe will bring you to tropical islands with its amazing flavor.

Preparation Time: 5 minutes
Total Time: 5 minutes
Yield: 2 servings

Ingredients

1 ½ cup fresh pineapple chunks
1 ½ jigger coconut cream
2 jigger white rum
1 cup crushed ice

Method

1. Combine the pineapple, coconut cream, and rum in a blender. Process until smooth. Add the crushed ice and blend further 20-30 seconds.
2. Pour in chilled glasses. Garnish with a small slice of pineapple and cherry, if desired.
3. Serve and enjoy.

♦♦♦♦♦♦♦♦♦

Pine-Orange Mai Tai Recipe

A perfect way to treat yourself on Friday nights. This cocktail has a great blend of flavors from the rum, pineapple juice, and orange juice.

Preparation Time: 5 minutes
Total Time: 5 minutes
Yield: 1 serving

Ingredients
1 jigger pineapple juice
1 jigger orange juice
½ jigger dark rum
½ jigger coconut-flavored rum
1 Tbsp. grenadine syrup
2/3 cup ice cubes

Method
1. Mix together pineapple juice, orange juice, dark rum, and coconut-flavored rum in a chilled glass. Add the ice cubes. Drizzle with grenadine. Do not stir. Garnish with a small slice of pineapple and cherry, if desired.
2. Serve and enjoy.

◆◆◆◆◆◆◆◆◆

Red Mai Tai Cocktail Recipe

This version of Mai Tai calls combines the flavor of rum, cranberry juice, and lime.

Preparation Time: 5 minutes
Total Time: 5 minutes
Yield: 2 servings

Ingredients

2 jiggers cran berry juice
1 jigger lime juice
1 jigger dark rum
½ jigger orange liqueur
½ jigger grenadine syrup
1 cup ice cubes

Method

1. Place the ice cubes, cranberry juice, lime juice, dark rum, orange liqueur, and grenadine in a cocktail shaker. Shake vigorously for 10-15 seconds.
2. Pour in chilled glasses including the ice. Garnish with mint sprig, if desired.
3. Serve and enjoy.

♦♦♦♦♦♦♦♦♦

Awesome Screwdriver Recipe

This classic cocktail recipe is very easy to make and only needs few basic ingredients.

Preparation Time: 5 minutes
Total Time: 5 minutes
Yield: 1 serving

Ingredients
½ cup fresh orange juice
¼ cup vodka
2/3 cup ice cubes
1 pc. sweet red cherry, for garnish

Method
1. Place the ice cubes, orange juice, and vodka in a cocktail shaker. Shake for 10-15 seconds.
2. Pour in a chilled glass including the ice. Garnish with cherry.
3. Serve and enjoy.

♦♦♦♦♦♦♦♦

The Original Long Island Iced Tea Recipe

You will not only enjoy making this fantastic drink, but will enjoy drinking it as well.

Preparation Time: 5 minutes
Total Time: 5 minutes
Yield: 2 servings

Ingredients
½ jigger rum
½ jigger gin
½ jigger vodka
½ jigger tequila
½ jigger triple sec
1 ½ jigger sweet and sour mix
1 ½ jigger cola
1 cup ice cubes
2 lemon slices

Method
1. Place the ice cubes, rum, gin, vodka, tequila, triple sec, sweet and sour mix, and cola in a cocktail shaker. Shake for 10-15 seconds.
2. Pour in chilled glasses including the ice. Add a slice of lemon.
3. Serve and enjoy.

♦♦♦♦♦♦♦♦

The Best Manhattan Cocktail Recipe

Rye whiskey is used in this recipe to replace the traditional Canadian whiskey because it gives a more flavorful cocktail.

Preparation Time: 5 minutes
Total Time: 5 minutes
Yield: 1 serving

Ingredients
1 ½ jigger rye whiskey
½ jigger sweet vermouth
2-3 dashes bitters
olives, for garnish

Method
1. Mix together the whiskey, vermouth, bitters, and ice cubes in a mixing glass. Stir to combine.
2. Strain and pour in a chilled glass. Garnish with olives.
3. Serve and enjoy.

♦♦♦♦♦♦♦♦♦

Easy Scotch Manhattan Cocktail Recipe

The classic Manhattan recipe with a twist. Scotch is used to replace whiskey. This cocktail is also called Rob Roy.

Preparation Time: 5 minutes
Total Time: 5 minutes
Yield: 1 serving

Ingredients

1 ½ jigger scotch
½ jigger sweet vermouth
2-3 dashes bitters
cherry, for garnish (optional)

Method

1. Mix together the scotch, vermouth, bitters, and ice cubes in a mixing glass. Stir to combine.
2. Strain and pour in a chilled glass. Garnish with cherry, if desired.
3. Serve and enjoy.

♦♦♦♦♦♦♦♦

Cocktails and More

The Ultimate Mojito Cocktail Recipe

This great tasting cocktail combines the flavor of rum, lime, and mint - a must try!

Preparation Time: 5 minutes
Total Time: 5 minutes
Yield: 2 servings

Ingredients

2 jiggers rum
1 Tbsp. simple syrup
½ lime, cut into thin wedges
½ cup lime-flavored soda water
6 pcs. mint leaves
1 cup ice cubes

Method

1. Mix together rum, syrup, lime, soda water, and mint leaves in a mixing glass. Stir to combine.
2. Divide and pour mixture into 2 chilled glasses over ice cubes.
3. Serve and enjoy.

◆◆◆◆◆◆◆◆

Perfect Lemon Mojito Cocktail Recipe

This mojito recipe with lemon is so refreshing and very delicious!

Preparation Time: 5 minutes
Total Time: 5 minutes
Yield: 2 servings

Ingredients

2 jiggers lemon-flavored rum
1 Tbsp. simple syrup
½ lemon, cut into thin wedges
½ cup carbonated water
6 pcs. mint leaves
1 cup ice cubes

Method

1. Mix together rum, syrup, lemon, carbonated water, and mint leaves in a mixing glass. Stir to combine.
2. Divide and pour mixture into 2 chilled glasses over ice cubes.
3. Serve and enjoy.

♦♦♦♦♦♦♦♦♦

Blue Hawaiian Cocktail Recipe

Take your regular cocktail to new heights by following this great tasting drink with pineapple juice, vodka, and blue curacao!

Preparation Time: 5 minutes
Total Time: 5 minutes
Yield: 2 servings

Ingredients
2 jigger pineapple juice
1 ½ jigger sweet and sour mix
1 ½ jigger vodka
½ jigger blue curacao
1 jigger lime juice
1 cup crushed ice

Method
1. Combine pineapple juice, sweet and sour mix, vodka, blue curacao, lime juice, and crushed ice in a blender. Process until smooth.
2. Pour in chilled glasses.
3. Serve and enjoy.

♦♦♦♦♦♦♦♦♦

Cool Blue Lagoon Cocktail Recipe

If you are looking for something that can cool you down when the weather is hot, then this is the recipe for you!

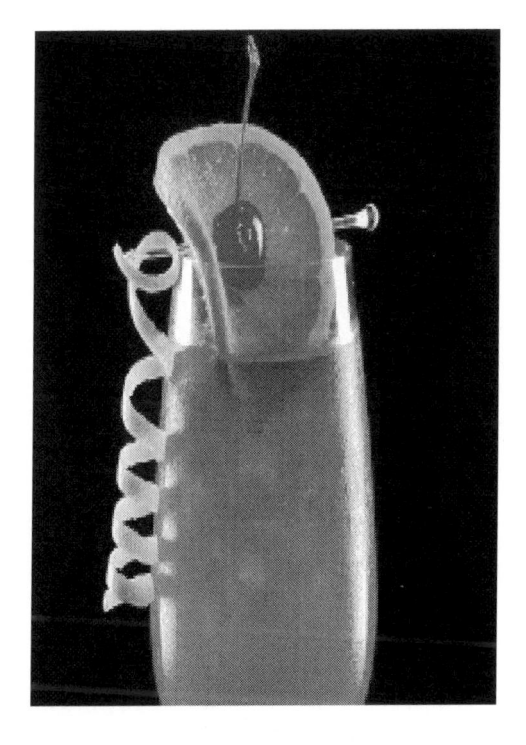

Preparation Time: 5 minutes
Total Time: 5 minutes
Yield: 2 servings

Ingredients
1 ½ jigger sweet and sour mix
1 ½ jigger tequila
½ jigger blue curacao
½ jigger lime juice
1 cup ice cubes

Method
1. Combine sweet and sour mix, tequila, blue curacao, and lime juice in a mixing glass. Stir well.
2. Pour in chilled glasses over ice cubes. Garnish with a slice of orange and cherry, if desired.
3. Serve and enjoy.

♦♦♦♦♦♦♦♦

Sexy Cosmopolitan Cocktail Recipe

This is the perfect party drink for girls, they will surely love it!

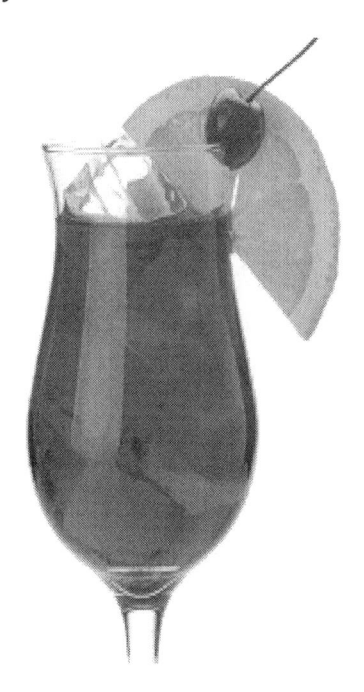

Preparation Time: 5 minutes
Total Time: 5 minutes
Yield: 2 servings

Ingredients
2 jiggers cranberry juice
2 jiggers vodka
½ cup soda water
½ jigger orange liqueur
1 cup ice cubes

Method
1. Combine the cranberry juice, vodka, soda water, and liqueur in a mixing glass. Stir well.
2. Pour in chilled glasses over ice cubes. Garnish with orange wedges and cherry, if desired.
3. Serve and enjoy.

♦♦♦♦♦♦♦♦♦

Peach Blossom Cocktail Recipe

If you got some peach schnapps and cranberry juice, try this awesome recipe!

Preparation Time: 5 minutes
Total Time: 5 minutes
Yield: 2 servings

Ingredients
1 jigger peach schnapps
1 jigger vodka
1 jigger cranberry juice
1 Tbsp. lime juice
1 Tbsp. triple sec
1 cup ice cubes

Method
1. Combine the peach schnapps, vodka, cranberry juice, lime juice, triple sec, and ice cubes in a mixing glass. Stir well.
2. Strain and pour in chilled glasses.
3. Serve and enjoy.

♦♦♦♦♦♦♦♦♦

Classic Bloody Mary Cocktail Recipe

If you want some spice in your drink, try this classic cocktail recipe that combines tomato juice, hot pepper, and vodka.

Preparation Time: 5 minutes
Total Time: 5 minutes
Yield: 1 serving

Ingredients
1 cup ice cubes
1 jigger vodka
¾ cup tomato-vegetable juice cocktail
1 tsp. Worcestershire sauce
1 tsp. hot pepper sauce
salt and pepper to taste
1 small stalk celery, for garnish

Method
1. Place the ice cubes, vodka, vegetable juice cocktail, Worcestershire sauce, and hot pepper sauce in a cocktail shaker. Season with salt and pepper to taste. Shake for 10-15 seconds.
2. Pour mixture in a chilled glass including the ice cubes. Garnish with celery stalk.
3. Serve and enjoy.

♦♦♦♦♦♦♦♦♦

Simple Daiquiri Cocktail Recipe

Sweet and simple, this cocktail recipe is a sure hit with the ladies.

Preparation Time: 5 minutes
Total Time: 5 minutes
Yield: 2 servings

Ingredients
1 ½ cup fresh strawberries
2 jigger rum
1 jigger simple syrup
½ jigger lime juice
1 cup crushed ice

Method
1. Combine strawberries, rum, syrup, and lime juice in a blender. Process until smooth. Add the crushed ice and blend further 20 seconds.
2. Pour in chilled glasses.
3. Serve and enjoy.

♦♦♦♦♦♦♦♦♦

Fresh Pineapple Daiquiri Recipe

This wonderful cocktail recipe has the taste of the tropics.

Preparation Time: 5 minutes
Total Time: 5 minutes
Yield: 2 servings

Ingredients
1 ½ cup fresh pineapple chunks
2 jigger rum
1 jigger simple syrup
½ jigger lemon juice
1 cup crushed ice

Method
1. Combine pineapple chunks, rum, syrup, and lemon juice in a blender. Process until smooth. Add the crushed ice and blend further 20 seconds.
2. Pour in chilled glasses.
3. Serve and enjoy.

♦♦♦♦♦♦♦♦

Easy Singapore Sling Recipe

There are many versions of this cocktail recipe but this one is the best!

Preparation Time: 5 minutes
Total Time: 5 minutes
Yield: 2 servings

Ingredients
2 jiggers pineapple juice
1 jigger gin
½ jigger cherry-flavored brandy
½ jigger orange liqueur
½ jigger triple sec
½ jigger lime juice
½ jigger grenadine
1 cup ice cubes

Method
1. Place the ice cubes, pineapple juice, gin, brandy, liqueur, triple sec, lime juice, grenadine, and ice cubes in a cocktail shaker. Shake for 10-15 seconds.
2. Strain and pour in chilled glasses. Garnish with cherry and strawberry, if desired.
3. Serve and enjoy.

◆◆◆◆◆◆◆◆◆

Easy Tom Collins Recipe

Another classic cocktail recipe with gin that is good to serve on any occasion.

Preparation Time: 5 minutes
Total Time: 5 minutes
Yield: 1 serving

Ingredients
1 jigger gin
½ jigger lemon juice
½ jigger simple syrup
¼ cup club soda
2/3 cup ice cubes
1 maraschino cherry, for garnish
2 pineapple chunks, for garnish

Method
1. Mix together gin, lemon juice, simple syrup, and club soda in a mixing glass.
2. Pour in a chilled glass with ice cubes. Garnish with cherry and pineapple chunks.
3. Serve and enjoy.

♦♦♦♦♦♦♦♦♦

Non-Alcoholic Cocktail Recipes

Pink Grapefruit and Pomegranate Cocktail Recipe

This sweet and tangy cocktail recipe makes a great refreshment any time of the day.

Preparation Time: 5 minutes
Total Time: 5 minutes
Yield: 2 servings

Ingredients
½ cup grapefruit juice
½ cup pomegranate juice
2 Tbsp. grenadine syrup
1 Tbsp. lime juice
1 cup crushed ice

Method
1. Combine the grapefruit juice, pomegranate juice, grenadine, lime juice, and crushed ice in a blender. Process until smooth.
2. Pour in chilled glasses. Garnish with a slice of grapefruit or lime, if desired.
3. Serve and enjoy.

♦♦♦♦♦♦♦♦

Orange Sunrise Cocktail Recipe

Enjoy summer with this cool and refreshing citrus drink!

Preparation Time: 5 minutes
Total Time: 5 minutes
Yield: 1 serving

Ingredients
½ cup orange juice
2 Tbsp. lemon juice
1 ½ Tbsp. grenadine syrup
2/3 cup ice cubes

Method
1. Mix together orange juice and lemon juice in a chilled glass. Add ice cubes and grenadine syrup let it settle at the bottom. Do not stir. Garnish with orange wedge, if desired.
2. Serve and enjoy.

◆◆◆◆◆◆◆◆

Cinnamon Spiced Orange Soda Cocktail Recipe

The flavor of cinnamon combines perfectly with the orange juice and soda in this delicious cocktail recipe.

Preparation Time: 5 minutes
Total Time: 5 minutes
Yield: 1 serving

Ingredients

½ cup orange juice
¼ cup soda water
1 Tbsp. simple syrup
1 Tbsp. lime juice
2/3 cup ice cubes
1 cinnamon stick
orange rind, thinly sliced

Method

1. Mix together orange juice, soda water, syrup, and lime juice in a chilled glass. Add ice cubes and cinnamon stick. Garnish with orange rind.
2. Serve and enjoy.

◆◆◆◆◆◆◆◆

Easy Orange Cranberry Cocktail Recipe

This pink cocktail with orange and cranberry juice is so easy to make and very delicious.

Preparation Time: 5 minutes
Total Time: 5 minutes
Yield: 1 serving

Ingredients
¼ cup orange juice
¼ cup cranberry juice
¼ cup soda water
1 Tbsp. simple syrup
2/3 cup ice cubes
orange wedge, for garnish
mint sprig, for garnish

Method
1. Mix together orange juice, cranberry juice, soda water, and syrup in a chilled glass. Add ice cubes. Garnish with orange wedge and mint sprig.
2. Serve and enjoy.

♦♦♦♦♦♦♦♦♦

Frozen Strawberry Pine and Lime Recipe

Beat the summer heat with this scrumptious red drink with strawberries, lime, and pineapple.

Preparation Time: 5 minutes
Total Time: 5 minutes
Yield: 2 servings

Ingredients
1 cup strawberries, halved
½ cup pineapple juice
1 Tbsp. lime juice
1 Tbsp. simple syrup
1cup crushed ice

Method
1. Combine strawberries, pineapple juice, lime juice, syrup, and crushed ice in a blender. Garnish with strawberry and lime wedge.
2. Serve and enjoy.

◆◆◆◆◆◆◆◆

Easy Lime Soda with Mint Cocktail Recipe

Stay hydrated with this refreshing drink made with lime juice, soda, and mint.

Preparation Time: 5 minutes
Total Time: 5 minutes
Yield: 1 serving

Ingredients
½ cup soda water
2 Tbsp. lime juice
1 Tbsp. simple syrup
½ cup ice cubes
4 mint leaves
4 lime wedges

Method
1. Mix together soda water, lime juice, syrup in a chilled glass. Add ice cubes, mint leaves, and lime wedges. Garnish with lime wedge and mint sprig, if desired
2. Serve and enjoy.

◆◆◆◆◆◆◆◆

Zesty Orange Cocktail with Mint Recipe

Got some oranges? Here is the perfect cocktail recipe for you!

Preparation Time: 5 minutes
Total Time: 5 minutes
Yield: 1 serving

Ingredients
½ cup orange juice
1 Tbsp. lime juice
1 Tbsp. simple syrup
2/3 cup ice cubes
2 mint leaves
2 lime wedges
1 orange wedge

Method
1. Mix together orange juice, lime juice, syrup, mint leaves and lime wedges in a chilled glass. Add ice cubes. Garnish with orange wedge, if desired
2. Serve and enjoy.

◆◆◆◆◆◆◆◆◆

Pomelo and Pineapple Cooler Recipe

This non-alcoholic cocktail recipe makes a great refreshment to any meal.

Preparation Time: 5 minutes
Total Time: 5 minutes
Yield: 2 servings

Ingredients

½ cup pomelo juice
½ cup pineapple juice
¼ cup soda water
2 Tbsp. simple syrup
1 cup ice cubes
2 pineapple chunks, for garnish
2 maraschino cherries, for garnish

Method

1. Stir together pomelo juice, pineapple juice, soda water, and grenadine syrup in a mixing glass.
2. Pour in chilled glasses with ice cubes. Garnish with pineapple chunks and cherries.
3. Serve and enjoy.

♦♦♦♦♦♦♦♦♦

Apple Grapefruit and Maple Cocktail Recipe

Here is a delicious treat when you need something to keep you refreshed.

Preparation Time: 5 minutes
Total Time: 5 minutes
Yield: 2 servings

Ingredients
½ cup apple juice
½ cup grapefruit juice
¼ cup soda water
2 Tbsp. maple syrup
1 cup ice cubes
apple slices, for garnish
mint sprig, for garnish

Method
1. Stir together apple juice, grapefruit juice, soda water, and maple syrup in a mixing glass.
2. Pour in chilled glasses with ice cubes. Garnish with apple slices and mint sprig.
3. Serve and enjoy.

♦♦♦♦♦♦♦♦

Mango Bravo Cocktail Recipe

This nice and sweet drink made of mango puree, orange, and soda is very delicious.

Preparation Time: 5 minutes
Total Time: 5 minutes
Yield: 2 servings

Ingredients
½ cup mango nectar or mango puree
½ cup orange juice
¼ cup soda water
1 cup ice cubes
2 orange wedges, for garnish
2 maraschino cherries, for garnish

Method
1. Stir together mango nectar, orange juice, and soda water in a mixing glass.
2. Pour in chilled glasses with ice cubes. Garnish with orange wedges and cherries.
3. Serve and enjoy.

◆◆◆◆◆◆◆◆

Cranberry Lime and Grenadine Cocktail Recipe

Treat yourself and your loved ones with this amazing cranberry-lime cocktail!

Preparation Time: 5 minutes
Total Time: 5 minutes
Yield: 2 servings

Ingredients
½ cup cranberry juice
¼ cup soda water
2 Tbsp. lime juice
2 Tbsp. grenadine syrup
1 cup ice cubes
2 lime wedges, for garnish

Method
1. Stir together cranberry juice, soda water, lime juice, and grenadine in a mixing glass.
2. Pour in chilled glasses with ice cubes. Garnish with lime wedges.
3. Serve and enjoy.

♦♦♦♦♦♦♦♦

Printed in Great Britain
by Amazon